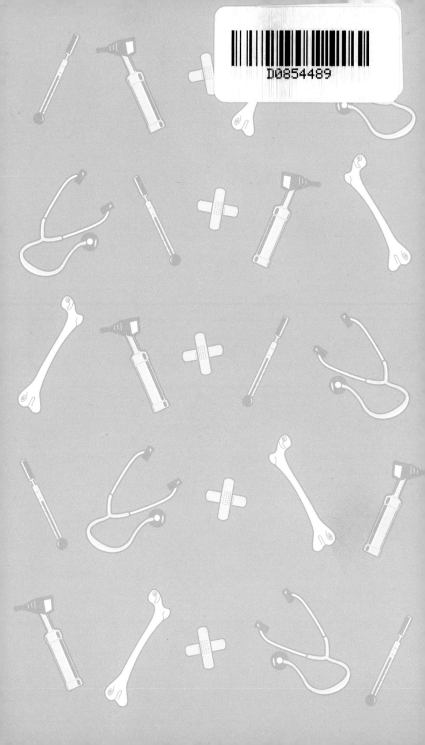

D0854489

OPERATION OUCH!

Your Brilliant Body

OPERATION OUCH!

Your Brilliant Body

Dr Chris van Tulleken
and
Dr Xand van Tulleken

LITTLE, BROWN BOOKS FOR YOUNG READERS
www.lbkids.co.uk

LITTLE, BROWN BOOKS FOR YOUNG READERS

First published in Great Britain in 2013 by Little, Brown Books for Young Readers
Reprinted 2013

Text copyright © 2013 by Maverick Television
Illustrations copyright © 2013 Hamyard

The moral right of the author has been asserted.

A CIP catalogue record for this book
is available from the British Library.

ISBN 978-0-349-00180-7

Printed and bound in Great Britain by
Clays Ltd, St Ives plc

Papers used by LBYR are from well-managed forests
and other responsible sources.

MIX
Paper from
responsible sources
FSC
www.fsc.org   FSC® C104740

Little, Brown Books for Young Readers
An imprint of
Little, Brown Book Group
100 Victoria Embankment
London EC4Y 0DY

An Hachette UK Company
www.hachette.co.uk

www.lbkids.co.uk

Contents

INTRODUCTION →

WELCOME TO OPERATION OUCH!

CHRIS: Hi! I'm Doctor Chris.

XAND: And I'm Doctor Xand.

CHRIS: We're twins, but it's very easy to tell us apart because I'm the cool one.

XAND: Actually, what Chris meant to say is that he THINKS he's the cool one. I hope that clears it up.

Chris **Xand**

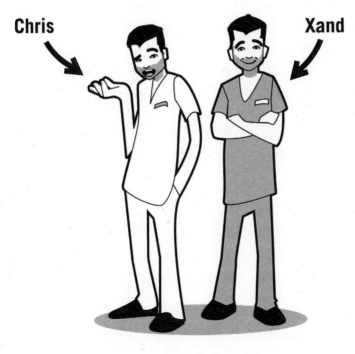

CHRIS: To prove how brilliant your body is, we're going to take you on a tour of it from nose hairs to toenails and everything in between.

XAND: Along the way we'll be sharing some startling facts. For example, did you know that your eye muscles will move almost 170 times a minute while you're reading this book?

CHRIS: So not only will you find out loads of amazing stuff, you'll also be giving your muscles a workout too. Sort of.

XAND: And be warned that we might possibly definitely gross you out. For example, we'll be telling you about how maggots and leeches are used in hospitals. I hope it doesn't put you off your dinner.

CHRIS: This won't be a problem if you're already eating maggots and leeches for your dinner, of course.

XAND: We'll also be showing you some amazing body tricks that will bamboozle your brain and astonish your friends. Some will even convince people that you've got super powers.

CHRIS: We're going to begin with the very things you're pointing at this page right now . . . Your eyes.

YOUR EYES →

CHRIS: Your eyes are amazing.

XAND: Thanks, Chris.

CHRIS: No, Xand, I meant everyone's eyes. They're one of the most complicated parts of the body.

Here's how your eyes work. You have a curved layer of skin on the front of your eyeball, which is called the cornea. The flexible disc behind it is called the lens. Together they bend rays of light to produce an image on the retina at the back of your eye.

When it appears on your retina, the image is actually upside down. But your brain turns it the right way up. Just like you did with this book.

CHRIS: The black bit in the middle of your eye is called your pupil. It's a hole to let light in. The coloured ring around the pupil is known as your iris.

XAND: The pattern of everyone's iris is unique. That's why irises are sometimes scanned in airports to check people's identity.

CHRIS: It's a bit like giving your fingerprint, except it makes you feel like you're in a cool sci-fi movie.

XAND: Above your eyeballs are your lacrimal glands, which produce tears. These wash over the surface of your eyes and help to protect against germs. Sometimes strong emotions increase the amount of tears they make, causing you to cry.

CHRIS: In Xand's case, this happens when he can't find his teddy bear, Mr Grumbles.

XAND: So what? He's a very sensitive bear. He gets worried when he's alone.

DID YOU KNOW?

People wear glasses if they are short-sighted and long-sighted. Short-sightedness can occur when an eyeball grows too long from front to back. Long-sightedness can occur when an eyeball is too short. Wearing glasses compensates for these eyeball shapes, and makes everyone assume you're clever.

People who have problems with their eyes sometimes have to be operated on by specialists. These surgeons are highly skilled.

The parts of the eye are so tiny and delicate that small instruments and fine needles and threads have to be used. Often the area being operated on has to be magnified to help the doctors see it.

GROSS OUT

About 50 per cent of people have tiny creatures living on their eyelashes. These eyelash mites are about a third of a millimetre long. They can sometimes cause allergic reactions, but most people never find out they've got them.

DID YOU KNOW?

Your eyes can process thirty-six thousand pieces of information an hour.

BODY TRICKS: Optical Illusion

CHRIS: Want to try a cool trick on yourself? Take a look at the reversed photo of me on page thirteen.

XAND: I think you'll find that's a picture of me.

CHRIS: No it isn't, but that's not important. Stare at it and count to thirty in your head. Then look away at a wall without blinking and you'll see an image of me.

XAND: No you won't. You'll see an image of me. But why does this happen?

CHRIS: At first, your eyes send messages about the picture to your brain. Soon they become tired and stop sending the messages, but your brain remembers them. When you look at the wall, your eyes send new messages, but it takes your brain a while to catch up. And that's why you continue to see the image.

XAND: Of me.

YOUR EARS →

CHRIS: Listen up, because the next stop on our tour of your brilliant body is your ears.

XAND: We'll tell you about the three different sections of it, and why earwax tastes so disgusting.

CHRIS: Although I'm sure you've never tried eating your own earwax. Never ever.

Although we refer to these flaps of skin and gristle on the side of our heads as our ears, they're really only the outer ear. We have to delve deeper into your head to find the rest of your ear.

The next part is the middle ear. The middle ear consists of the eardrum and three small bones called the ossicles. And finally the inner ear. The inner ear consists of the cochlear and semi-circular canals. Your inner ear contains fluid that sends information to your brain about balance and movement.

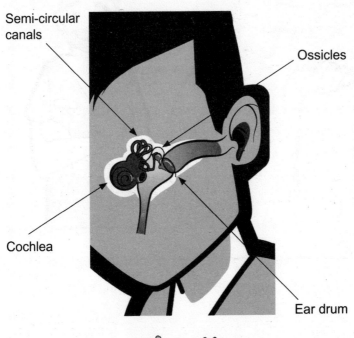

Semi-circular canals

Ossicles

Cochlea

Ear drum

This fluid is the reason you sometimes get travel sick. When you're looking out of a car window, your eyes tell your brain that your body is moving. But because you're actually sitting still, the fluid in your ears tells your brain you're not moving. Talk about mixed messages!

As a result, your brain gets confused and you might start to feel queasy. Some people are more sensitive to this than others, so not everyone gets travelsick.

GROSS OUT

Earwax is produced by your body to protect the lining of your ear canal by trapping dirt and repelling water. By the time it reaches the outer ear, it's been inside your ear for about a month. No wonder it tastes so disgusting.

CHRIS: If you ever find yourself feeling sick, there's a very simple solution to the problem.

XAND: That's right. Just grab your twin brother's rucksack and spew up in there.

CHRIS: What? No! I was going to say that you should look out of the window at a fixed spot on the horizon. That way neither your eyes nor your ears will think you're moving so both will send the same messages to your brain, and it won't get confused.

XAND: Oh. Right. Sorry about your rucksack.

Humans can hear a wide range of sounds, although the range narrows as you get older. So if you can hear a noise that your parents can't, it's because they're old and you're young. Or maybe it's because you've got your headphones on.

Your ears are very sensitive, so it's important not to shove anything into them, like stones or chickpeas. (Believe us, we've seen it all on *Operation Ouch!*)

If something gets stuck in your ear, it can sometimes cause infections. So no matter how much you want to block out the sound of your brother, sister, mum, dad or teacher, don't put anything into your ear!

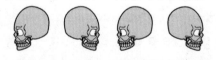

THAT'S BRILLIANT

Indian grocer Radhakant Baijpal has the longest ear hairs in the world. He has thick black hairs measuring up to twenty-five centimetres growing out of each ear. He washes his tufts with a special herbal shampoo.

DID YOU KNOW?

Dogs have a greater range of hearing than humans. Dog whistles emit high frequency sounds that can't be heard by us. So if you've ever heard one it means you're a dog and not a human. And in that case you should probably be running around the park instead of reading a book. Walkies!

BODY TRICKS: Super Strength

CHRIS: Here's a trick to convince your friends you've got super strength.

XAND: I don't need to use it because I've already got super strength.

CHRIS: Xand, if you've got super strength, why did I have to help you get the lid off that jar of pickled onions the other day?

XAND: Er . . .

CHRIS: Anyway, here's what to do. Get a friend to sit on a chair in front of you, with their back to a wall. They need to rest the back of their head against the wall and place their arms on their lap. Press your finger against their forehead and ask them to stand up.

XAND: They won't be able to, and they'll think you're amazingly strong. Just like I am.

CHRIS: The truth is, it's got nothing to do with super strength and everything to do with the balance that your ears give you. When you're getting up from a chair, you need to lean forward and shift your weight to your legs. If you can't lean forward, you can't stand up. Try it!

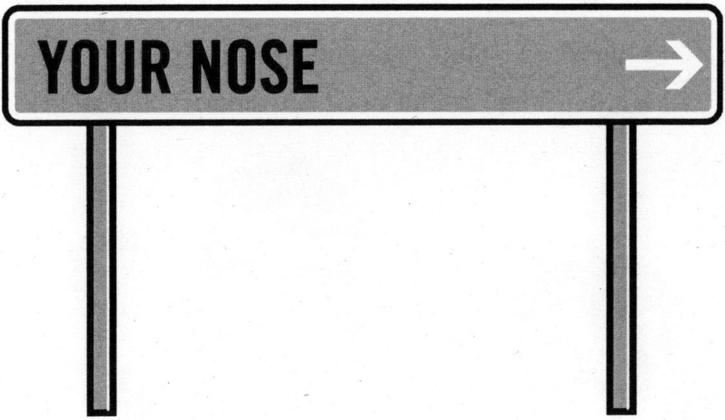
YOUR NOSE

CHRIS: We were having a bit of trouble choosing which part of your brilliant body to delve into next.

XAND: We've decided to pick your nose.

CHRIS: Which is something you should never do, of course.

XAND: But it does taste nice.

CHRIS: That's a matter of opinion, Xand!

QUIZ

How much snot does the average person produce in a year?

A. Enough to fill one fish tank.
B. Enough to fill two bathtubs.
C. Enough to fill three teapots.

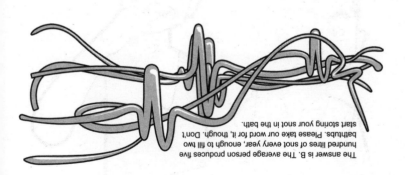

The answer is B. The average person produces five hundred litres of snot every year, enough to fill two bathtubs. Please take our word for it, though. Don't start storing your snot in the bath.

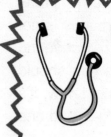

DID YOU KNOW?

Your nose can detect over ten thousand different scents.

You breathe in air through your nose, which warms, filters and moistens the air before it travels down to your lungs. All the little hairs that line your nostrils help to keep out dust.

Behind your nostrils is a large area called the nasal cavity. This is lined with mucus. Lovely. Mucus is a sticky fluid that moistens air and traps germs. You could probably find some dried nasal mucus in your nostrils right now, if you really wanted to look.

Yes, we're talking about bogies. They're pretty gross, and calling them dried nasal mucus is not going to change that. If you've been wondering why your bogies taste so salty, then you should probably get out more. But if you must know, it's because snot contains lots of chemicals, and one of them is salt.

Around your nasal cavity there are air-filled spaces called sinuses. No one knows exactly what they're for, though some scientists think they might help to control temperature, or to make your skull lighter.

Whatever they're for, sinuses can become a real nuisance if they get blocked. If this happens it can make it hard to breathe, or cause snot to leak out of your nose. Eww!

CHRIS: The most important use of your nose is so that you can smell things. But have you ever wondered *why* you smell?

XAND: Is it because odour detectors in your nasal cavity send information to smell centres in your brain?

CHRIS: No. It's because you don't shower enough.

XAND: I walked right into that one, didn't I?

We all know that sneezes can be gooey and unpleasant for you and the person sitting in front of you on the bus. But did you know that sneezes have less to do with your nose than you might think? When you sneeze, saliva sprays out of your *mouth*, but nothing comes out of your nose.

It's only *after* you sneeze that mucus runs down your nose to flush out whatever caused the irritation.

Your nose, mouth and stomach are all closely connected. This is why sick sometimes comes out of your nose as well as your mouth when you're throwing up. *Bleurgh!*

Sometimes this connection can be very useful, because if a patient is too ill to eat, doctors push a nasogastric tube up their nose. Ouch! The tube passes through the nasal cavity, down the throat and into the stomach. Liquid food is then poured down the tube. Yum.

GROSS OUT

Nasal mucus, also known as snot, might be the most famous type, but lots of other bits of your body produce mucus too, including your mouth, lungs, bum and eyes. Mucus protects you from germs in all the places where they could get into your body.

QUIZ

How far does your digestive system stretch?

A. The length of a car.
B. The height of a three-storey building.
C. All the way to the moon.

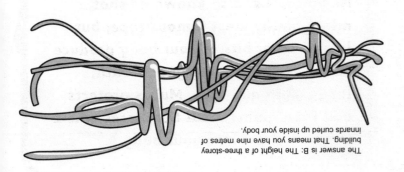

The answer is B: The height of a three-storey building. That means you have nine metres of innards curled up inside your body.

BODY TRICKS: Lifting a Finger

CHRIS: Here's an amazing body trick that will stop your friends being able to move their fingers.

XAND: They won't be able to use their fingers any more? That sounds quite dangerous.

CHRIS: Not permanently, just for the trick. Here's how it goes. Fold your middle finger under your palm and place your hand palm-down on a table. Can you move your little finger?

XAND: Yep.

CHRIS: Can you move your thumb?

XAND: Yep.

CHRIS: Can you move your index finger?

XAND: Yep.

CHRIS: Can you move your ring finger?

XAND: Hang on . . . wait a minute . . . almost there . . .

CHRIS: No, you can't. That's because all your fingers have separate muscles except for your middle finger and your ring finger. The muscles that move these are connected, so when your middle finger is folded down, you can't move your ring finger.

XAND: Give me a minute . . . I've nearly done it.

CHRIS: You can stop trying now, Xand. The trick's over.

YOUR MOUTH →

CHRIS: Can you remember which bit of the body we're dealing with next, Xand?

XAND: It's on the tip of my tongue . . .

CHRIS: Correct.

Your Tongue

For its size, the tongue is the strongest muscle in the human body.

It's covered with about ten thousand taste buds and inside each of these there are up to one hundred cells helping you taste everything from the sweetest cake to the spiciest chilli.

Every time you eat or drink something, taste buds send messages to your brain about it. If it's an apple, your brain will probably tell you to go ahead and take a bite. If it's a raw onion, your brain will probably tell you to cook it first. Unless you like eating raw onions. Who are we to judge?

THAT'S BRILLIANT

Stephen Taylor from Coventry has the world's longest tongue. It measures ten centimetres from tip to lip, which means the whole thing is as long as a Cumberland sausage. It's so long he can even eat a yoghurt without using a spoon, which must save on the washing up.

Your sense of taste works closely with your sense of smell to determine overall flavour. This is why food sometimes tastes different when you have a cold – it's because your nose is blocked and doesn't work properly.

Tastes can be sweet, sour, salty, bitter or umami. Umami refers to the strong savoury flavour of foods like cheese, meat and fish. You could experience all these tastes at once if you made yourself a cheese and lemon sandwich covered with sugar, salt and vinegar. But don't. It would be disgusting.

Taste buds aren't just found on your tongue. They're also on the inside of your cheeks, the roof of your mouth and your lips. But wherever they are, you should be grateful to them. Without them, the tastiest sweets, the freshest fruits and the most delicious pizzas would all taste as horrible as the mouldy school dinner scrapings in the bins at the back of the playground.

DID YOU KNOW?

Hot chillies contain a substance called capsaicin. Capsaicin triggers the pain detectors on your tongue. This is why hot food sometimes gives you a burning sensation in your mouth. Some people avoid this painful experience at all costs, while others enjoy it and develop a taste for spicy foods.

XAND: As you get older, some of your taste buds die, and they are not replaced.

CHRIS: This means that younger people can be more sensitive to taste than older people.

XAND: Although that probably isn't a good enough excuse to leave the parts of your dinner you don't like.

DID YOU KNOW?

Your tongue print is as unique as your fingerprint. It's just as well the police chose fingerprints as the standard way to identify people, though. It wouldn't be very nice to have to dip your tongue in ink and lick a piece of paper.

QUIZ

How much spit does the average human produce in a lifetime?

A. Enough to fill five hundred bathtubs.
B. Enough to flush a toilet with.
C. Enough to pour over your cereal at breakfast.

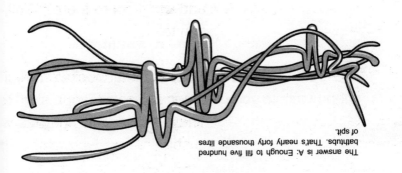

The answer is A: Enough to fill five hundred bathtubs. That's nearly forty thousand litres of spit.

BODY TRICKS: Tricking Your Taste Buds

CHRIS: Did you know it's possible to fool your taste buds?

XAND: You have to start by closing your eyes and sticking your tongue out.

CHRIS: Obviously, this would be very rude in some situations, such as school assemblies and royal visits.

XAND: But it's fine for the purposes of this experiment.

CHRIS: Make sure your tongue is completely dry.

XAND: Then get a friend to place a piece of food on your tongue without telling you what it is.

CHRIS: It's important that you chose a trustworthy friend to help you with this experiment.

XAND: And not someone who finds the idea of putting mud on your tongue hilarious.

CHRIS: Try and guess what the food on your tongue is.

XAND: You probably won't be able to. This is because the molecules that give food flavour need to dissolve in saliva before you can detect them. Without saliva, food doesn't seem to have a taste at all.

CHRIS: Now put your tongue back into your mouth, let your saliva do its thing, and find out what the food was.

XAND: I hope for your sake it's something pleasant rather than a piece of rotting cabbage your friend found at the back of the fridge.

Your Teeth

CHRIS: While we're looking into your mouth, we should spend a bit of time examining your teeth.

XAND: Luckily for you, we're doctors, not dentists. So we won't be following the examination by drilling into your teeth.

CHRIS: Or making you spit blood-filled saliva into a little basin.

XAND: Now say 'aah' . . .

A strange thing about teeth is that you get two different sets in your life. First, there are the twenty baby teeth, or milk teeth, that appear by the age of about three. Then there are the thirty-two adult teeth that start to replace them when you're six or seven.

We're all so used to this that it's easy to forget how odd it is. After all, we don't find our arms dropping off when we're six and having to wait for new ones to grow. And we don't casually pull our ears off and stick them under the pillow for the ear fairy.

Another weird thing about your teeth is that you don't even get a complete set until you're quite old. The last ones to grow are the four molars at the very back of your mouth. These don't emerge until you're between sixteen and twenty-five.

These teeth are known as your wisdom teeth because they don't grow until you're old, and old people are supposed to be wiser, for some reason.

Your Throat

CHRIS: The next stop on our tour of your brilliant body is your throat, a passageway for both food and air.

XAND: Your body usually does a brilliant job of separating the two, but sometimes they can get mixed up.

There are two tubes leading down from your throat. One of them is called the windpipe and it goes to your lungs. The other is called the oesophagus and it goes to your stomach.

Sometimes a bit of food might go down your windpipe by mistake, which can be very nasty. If you're lucky, you'll find yourself coughing the food up into your mouth. It might be a bit gross, but at least you'll be safe.

Your Tonsils

XAND: Also at the back of your throat are your mysterious tonsils.

CHRIS: It's not just *your* tonsils that are mysterious, by the way. All tonsils are. Even experts like us don't know exactly what they do. And we've looked it up in a book and everything.

XAND: Doctors are pretty sure that they help us fight germs, though they don't know exactly how.

Your tonsils are at the back of your throat. When they're helping to fight germs, they might swell and become uncomfortable. This is called tonsillitis.

Sometimes tonsils become so inflamed that a doctor has to remove them. Luckily, this is a very straightforward operation, and there are plenty of other bits of your body that will help you fight infections after your tonsils have gone.

Healthy Tonsils

Inflamed Tonsils

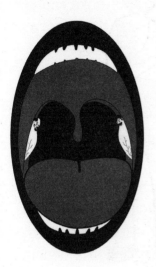
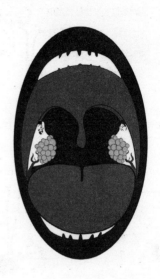

Your Voice Box

XAND: There was just one more thing I wanted to include in this chapter. What was it?

CHRIS: I'll give you a clue. You're using it right now.

XAND: My novelty furry pencil case?

CHRIS: No – your voice box.

51

Your voice box is technically called your larynx and it's found at the top of your windpipe. It's used when you sing, shout, whisper and make random squeaking noises to annoy your brothers and sisters on long car journeys.

Your voice box houses your vocal cords, which are a bit like elastic bands. When the muscles attached to them move, their shape changes, altering the sounds that come out of your mouth.

Men usually have bigger vocal cords than women, which is why they have deeper voices. When boys hit their teenage years, their vocal cords become thicker, causing their voices to 'break'. Sometimes boys find their voices going unexpectedly croaky or squeaky while it happens, which can be rather embarrassing.

Everyone's voice is unique. No one has a voice like yours. It's created by a combination of your larynx, mouth and nose. This unique combination is what makes some people have brilliant singing voices that can captivate millions, while others should probably stick to singing in the shower.

YOUR BRAIN →

CHRIS: You have the most powerful computer in the world right inside your skull.

XAND: So next time someone shows off their swanky new smartphone or games console, you can tell them you've got something better inside your head.

CHRIS: But rather than a sleek chrome rectangle, you brain is a pink squidgy blob.

XAND: Which wouldn't look very good in the window of your local computer shop.

Your teachers and older siblings might think they've got brilliant brains, but the truth is that so do you. In fact, everyone does. All our brains are stuffed full of facts, memories and dreams, and are constantly crackling with tiny pulses of electricity. They're brilliantly complicated machines that scientists are only just beginning to understand.

Your brain is a soft and floppy organ that's protected by hard bone, soft membranes and cushioning fluid. And it's no wonder it needs to be packaged so carefully. It's the most precious part of your body, and keeping it safe couldn't be more important.

BRAIN PUTER

QUIZ

How many dreams does the average person have in a year?

- A. The same as the number of baked beans in a tin.
- B. The same as the number of miles from Newcastle to Rome.
- C. The same as the number of planes that leave Heathrow Airport each day.

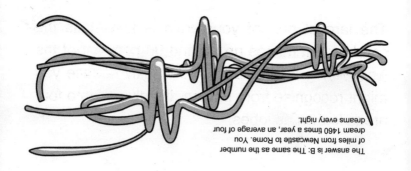

The answer is B: The same as the number of miles from Newcastle to Rome. You dream 1460 times a year, an average of four dreams every night.

Your Cranium

The bone around your brain is called the cranium. It's evolved to be tough enough to safeguard your brain if something knocks your head. Hair and skin add additional protection, but there are times – whether you're riding a bike, playing cricket or flying a plane as part of an aerial display team – when you'll need to wear a helmet too.

Your Cerebrum

The largest part of your brain is known as the cerebrum. It makes up around 90 per cent of the whole thing and includes the wrinkly surface you might recognise from photos. It's divided into four areas known as lobes.

CHRIS: Each lobe is associated with different functions. The frontal lobe is involved with speech and movement.

XAND: The parietal lobe helps us interpret things like touch.

CHRIS: The occipital lobe at the back helps with sight.

XAND: And the temporal lobes on either side helps with . . . Er . . . Hang on a minute . . . It'll come back to me . . .

CHRIS: Memory, Xand. They help with memory.

XAND: Wait! I've got it! The temporal lobes help with memory.

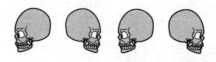

QUIZ

How many calculations can the average human brain perform in one second?

A. Ten thousand
B. Ten quadrillion
C. One

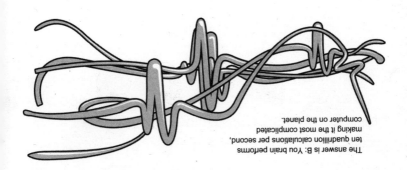

The answer is B: Your brain performs ten quadrillion calculations per second, making it the most complicated computer on the planet.

Your Left and Right Brain

The brain is also divided into two halves. It's often said that the left side is involved with scientific thought, while the right side is associated with artistic skills.

So according to this theory, if you looked at a flower, the left side of your brain might wonder what the different parts of it were called. Whereas the right side of your brain might want to write a poem about it. Obviously the reality is a lot more complicated than this, but it's true that the two halves of your brain work differently.

Your Cerebellum

A wrinkled lump at the back of your brain is known as the cerebellum. It helps to send signals from your brain to your muscles. So if you miss a penalty while playing football, blame it on your cerebellum and your teammates will understand.

XAND: What is a thought? What is a memory? What is a dream?

CHRIS: Are you feeling all right, Xand? Do you need to lie down?

XAND: I'm fine. I'm just saying that these are all important questions to do with our brains and how they work. Scientists are only just beginning to work out the answers to some of them.

CHRIS: Weirdo.

Your brain consists of billions of tiny cells called neurons. As you learn new things, your brain creates pathways between them so you can access them as memories.

These links stay strong if you continue to think about the things you've learned, but fade if you don't. This is why some things stay in your memory for a long time, while others slip your mind. It's not a good idea to use this as an excuse if you forget your best friend's birthday, though.

Another thing your brain does is dream. We know dreams occur during a period called REM (Rapid Eye Movement) sleep. During these times our breathing speeds up and our eyes move beneath their lids.

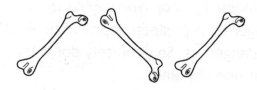

Sleep

CHRIS: All this talk about dreams is making me drowsy. I might have a nap.

XAND: That's another strange thing about the brain. It seems to want to switch off at the end of the day.

CHRIS: But what exactly is sleep?

THAT'S BRILLIANT

A woman called Maureen Weston of Peterborough was recorded as going for eighteen days and seventeen hours without sleep in 1977. However, the *Guinness Book of World Records* no longer records sleep deprivation, as it's so dangerous. So definitely don't try that one at home.

On average, we spend a third of our lives sleeping. Although it might seem as though our brains have shut down like a computer, they actually remain active during sleep. Important processes like mending cells occur while we're asleep. This is one of the reasons why it's so important to get enough sleep.

Newborn babies sleep for about twenty hours a day, but by the time we reach adulthood, we tend to need between seven and eight hours. It varies a lot, however. Some people only need a few hours sleep every night, which means they can do jobs with unusual hours.

But for most people, sleeping for fewer than seven hours will cause headaches, confusion and slow reactions. As you'll know if you've ever been woken up early by your little sister jumping on the bed.

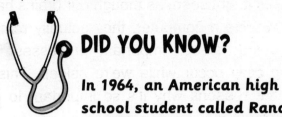

DID YOU KNOW?

In 1964, an American high school student called Randy Gardner stayed awake for over eleven days as part of a study. It was found that he suffered from mood swings, paranoia and hallucinations. After a while, he started to believe he wasn't a student at all, but a famous American football player.

BODY TRICKS: Hot and Cold Water

CHRIS: Here's a trick that will let you confuse your friend's brain just by using three bowls of water.

XAND: Fill one of the bowls with cold water, one of the bowls with lukewarm water and one of the bowls with hot water.

CHRIS: That's hot water from the tap like you'd have in the bath, and not boiling water from the kettle, by the way. You're supposed to trick your friend's brain, not burn their hands.

XAND: Get them to put one hand in the cold water and one hand in the hot water and leave them for a minute. You can pretend to work your magic powers on them while you're waiting if you like. It's up to you.

CHRIS: Now get them to put both their hands into the lukewarm water.

XAND: One of their hands will tell them the water is boiling hot, while the other will tell them it's freezing cold. And yet they'll be able to see with their own eyes that it's the same water.

CHRIS: If your friend is actually an alien robot who's only pretending to be human, their brain will explode at this point.

XAND: And well done you for exposing one of those sneaky robots.

CHRIS: Why the confusion? It's because your nerves measure the temperature of the water in relation to the temperature of your hand. If the water's warmer than your hand, it feels warm. And if the water's colder than your hand, it feels cold.

XAND: The trick works even if you know it's going to happen.

CHRIS: Try it on yourself if you like.

XAND: Unless you're an alien robot too. You're not, are you?

DID YOU KNOW?

Your collarbone is the last of your bones to stop growing when you become an adult. It's called the clavicle and it won't stop growing until you're about twenty-five.

As we've seen, the brain is an incredibly complicated part of your body, so doctors who specialise in it have to be highly skilled.

CHRIS: It's so complex that we even use the expression 'It's not brain surgery' to describe something that *isn't* difficult.

XAND: Luckily the expression 'It's not rocket science' also exists, so brain surgeons can describe simple things too.

Brain surgeons use special saws and drills to open a flap in the bone to get to the brain. Then they use long thin instruments if they need to remove parts of it. Ouch!

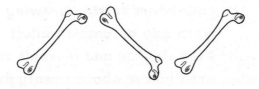

CHRIS: We've probably all had a headache at one point or another.

XAND: They quite often get better on their own if you drink plenty of water and go to bed.

CHRIS: Listening to a heavy metal album at full volume, on the other hand, won't help.

The pain you feel when you get a headache actually comes from the parts around your brain, such as the blood vessels. Amazingly, the brain itself can't feel pain at all. Changes in temperature, pressure, or even damage to brain tissue would not be detected by your brain.

This can prove useful during brain surgery. The lack of pain sometimes allows patients to remain conscious during the entire procedure!

YOUR NERVES →

CHRIS: Now it's time for us to get on your nerves.

XAND: Are you sure, Chris? We don't want to annoy anyone, do we?

CHRIS: No, I mean we should get on to the next section, which is about nerves.

XAND: Oh. I see.

QUIZ

How many kilometres of nerves run through your skin?

A. Seventy kilometres
B. Forty-five kilometres
C. Twenty kilometres

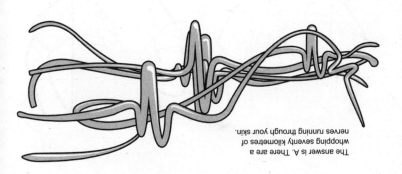

The answer is A. There are a whopping seventy kilometres of nerves running through your skin.

Clever as your brain is, it wouldn't be able to do much without the network of nerves that link it to the rest of your body. Nerves bring information from your senses to your brain and deliver orders from your brain to the other bits of your body.

There are many major nerves in your body. Some of these are called cranial nerves and they join your brain to places such as your eyes, nose, tongue, ears, heart and lungs.

Another major nerve is your spinal cord, which links your brain to the rest of your body. It has pairs of smaller nerves branching off it that connect to muscles, blood vessels and other body parts.

Your spinal cord and your brain are known as your central nervous system. They're vital parts of your body, so you should never pull them out through your ears to have a look at them. No matter how curious you are.

Nerves are very delicate. If they are damaged they are very slow to mend. Some people damage their nerves in accidents, and have to wait a long time for them to regrow all their complex connections.

Sometimes the spinal cord sends signals back to muscles without even involving the brain. The reactions that occur are known as reflexes and they include blinking, sneezing, blushing,

yawning and pulling your hand away from something that's too hot. A very famous reflex is the knee-jerk. This happens when you tap the area just below your kneecap to make your lower leg jolt up.

CHRIS: **We've probably all experienced a minor nerve problem called pins and needles at some point.**

XAND: That's the name for the strange numb feeling we get when we've been doing something like kneeling down for too long.

CHRIS: It happens because you've cut off the blood supply to the nerves in a certain part of your body. In Xand's case, his lower legs.

XAND: Pins and needles usually goes away quite quickly.

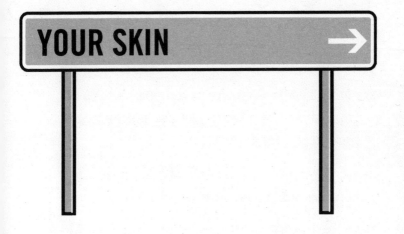

XAND: Take a look at the person nearest to you. Amazingly, what you are seeing is not technically alive.

CHRIS: Aaarrghh! I knew it! There's been a zombie outbreak! Run for the hills!

XAND: Not quite. It's because the layer of skin you can see is actually made of small dead flakes. The living layer of skin is below the surface.

CHRIS: Phew!

The outer layer of your skin is called the epidermis and consists of dead cells that provide protection from dirt and germs. Your body is constantly losing and replacing these cells.

Your dead skin cells sometimes absorb water and swell. This is the reason the ends of your fingers go wrinkly in the bath. Your skin also contains natural oils that repel water, so fortunately you won't swell up like a huge sponge if you spend too long in there.

DID YOU KNOW?

Areas of skin that endure lots of friction can form tough patches called calluses. For example, someone who plays the guitar will form calluses on their fingertips.

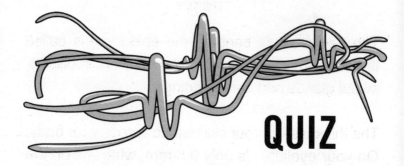

QUIZ

How much does the average adult's skin weigh?

A. The same as one pug dog.
B. The same as two newborn babies.
C. The same as three pineapples.

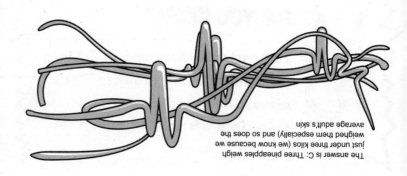

The answer is C: Three pineapples weigh just under three kilos (we know because we weighed them especially) and so does the average adult's skin

The thicker layer beneath the epidermis is called the dermis and contains blood vessels, hair follicles, sweat glands and nerve endings.

The thickness of your skin varies across your body. On your eyelids, it's only 0.5 mm, whereas on the soles of your feet, it can be as thick as 5 mm.

If you took your skin off and stretched it over the ground, it would cover about two square metres. That's enough to use as a picnic blanket. But don't be tempted to try it. It would be very painful for you and attract flies to your picnic.

DID YOU KNOW?

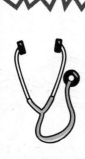

The entire surface of your skin is replaced every month. That's almost one thousand new skins in a lifetime.

Skin Injuries

CHRIS: The doctors in your local hospital spend a lot of time treating cuts and wounds.

XAND: But they don't deserve all the credit, because skin is amazing at healing itself.

CHRIS: But make sure you don't *just* thank your skin and not your doctor if you get a wound treated, though. That would be rude.

Minor cuts and scratches are very common, and your skin heals these by producing extra cells. A lump called a clot forms to stop blood from leaking out and dirt and germs from getting in. The clot hardens into a tough scab while a new layer of skin forms underneath. When the new skin is complete, the scab dries and falls off.

How many bruises have you got? You might have banged yourself playing football, skating or falling off your bike, but did you know that a bruise is actually trapped blood?

Sometimes blood vessels under your skin leak even though the skin itself doesn't break. The blood gets trapped under your skin and goes through a rancid rainbow of colours as it heals – black, blue, crimson, yellow and green. Nice.

DID YOU KNOW?

Scientists can grow artificial skin from a healthy piece taken from a patient. It's used to help people who've suffered skin damage or severe burns. Doctors place the lab-grown skin on damaged areas to help speed up the healing process.

Have you ever had a blister? If so, you'll know how painful they can be. But do you know what they are and why they're there? Well, we're doctors, so we can tell you.

They're small pockets of fluid that form when the outer layers of your skin have been damaged. They act like your body's own version of a plaster, cushioning and protecting the tissue beneath a damaged layer of skin. So it's not actually the blister that's causing the pain, it's the damaged skin underneath.

Though it can be very tempting to pop your blisters and let all the wonderfully disgusting goo out, it's much better to leave them alone so your body can absorb the fluid. Sorry.

GROSS OUT

Sometimes maggots are used to help people with serious wounds. Medical maggots are bred in sterile environments so they're completely free of germs. These maggots are used to eat dead skin away from large wounds, allowing them to heal. They're like tiny, blind, legless surgeons. Maybe we should make them some white coats.

QUIZ

How much skin will you shed in your lifetime?

A. Enough to sprinkle on your fish and chips.
B. Enough to fill a two storey house.
C. None, because you're not a snake.

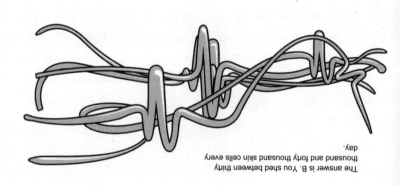

The answer is B. You shed between thirty thousand and forty thousand skin cells every day.

Your Skin and Temperature

CHRIS: What gives you goose bumps and makes your hair stand on end?

XAND: Vampires. Werewolves. Ghosts. Losing Mr Grumbles.

CHRIS: Really? It happens to me when I'm cold and the blood vessels near the surface of my skin get narrower.

XAND: Yeah, me too. That's what I meant to say.

Your skin plays a very important role in keeping your body at a regular temperature. Humans need to stay at around thirty-seven degrees Celsius, and the skin has a few tricks to help maintain this temperature.

When you're hot, the blood vessels near the surface of your skin widen, increasing the flow of blood to your skin and taking heat away from the rest of your body. The opposite happens when you're cold. The blood vessels get narrower, decreasing the flow of blood to your skin from your body.

This is because your body is making a choice. It's taking blood away from the parts it can do without such as your fingers and toes (after all, you've got ten of each!) and pulling it to the vital organs it needs to stay alive, such as your brain and your heart.

In response, the hairs on your skin stand up to trap heat next to your body. Tiny muscles pull the hairs up and cause goose bumps. It's called goose bumps because it makes your skin look like that of a goose.

Goose bumps also occur when you're frightened or stressed. This is an automatic reflex, similar to when the quills of porcupines and the hairs of cats stand on end. For those animals, the reflex helps them look bigger to scare away predators.

Some people think goose bumps are from when humans were much furrier and could scare attackers away by puffing our hairs up and making ourselves seem bigger. But others think it's because your body draws heat to your muscles to make sure you're ready to attack. In this theory, your hairs rise up to trap heat.

So if you're watching a scary film and find your hairs standing up, it's either because you're about to attack your TV, or you think it will be more frightened of you if you look bigger. Both of which are a bit silly.

YOUR HAIR →

CHRIS: We all know that pop stars care a lot about their hair.

XAND: But we should too.

CHRIS: Just because we don't spend three hours a day combing and spraying our hair, it doesn't mean we shouldn't appreciate it.

The number of hairs on your head ranges from around ninety thousand to one-hundred and forty thousand, depending on what sort of hair you have. People with fair hair have the most, followed by people with dark hair, followed by people with red hair.

Everyone loses about fifty to one hundred hairs every day, but this process can speed up in men as they get older, causing their hair to thin out. If this is happening to your dad, please encourage him to go for the cool shaved head look rather than the comb-over, which involves sweeping chunks of hair over a bald patch.

Your eyebrows are thin patches of hair that stop sweat and rain from flowing into your eyes. They also help to communicate emotions like surprise and anger. So don't shave them off. Not only will your eyes get blinded with sweat, but you won't be able to show everyone how angry you are about it.

THAT'S BRILLIANT

Sam 'Hairy' Smith is Britain's hairiest man. He's covered in thick body hair, which measures up to fifteen centimetres. He has to use four towels to dry himself after every shower.

Hair grows from pits in the skin known as follicles. The roots of these are the only living parts of your hair. The hair we see above the skin is already dead.

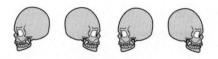

If you don't cut your hair, it will most likely stop growing when it's about 1.5 metres long. But some people can grow their hair even longer. The current world record for longest hair is 5.6 metres. We don't recommending trying to beat this, as you'll probably end up tripping over your hair and having to pay us a visit in the hospital.

As well as the hair on your scalp, you have millions of soft, tiny hairs covering your body. They play an important role in keeping your body the right temperature – as we talked about in the Your Skin chapter.

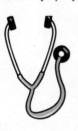

DID YOU KNOW?

Human hair feels soft, but it's one of the strongest fibres on the planet.

QUIZ

How much sweat does the average adult produce in a year?

- A. Enough to fill a large water pistol.
- B. Enough to fill a bucket.
- C. Enough to fill a family car.

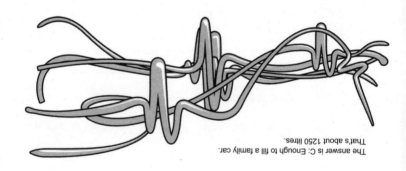

The answer is C: Enough to fill a family car. That's about 1250 litres.

YOUR BONES →

CHRIS: You've got a lot to thank your skeleton for.

XAND: Without it, you'd just be a floppy mass of skin, blood and muscles.

CHRIS: And then what would you do when your teachers told you to stop slouching?

Your skeleton is made up of 206 bones, including your collarbone, breastbone, upper arms, forearms, ribs, hip bone, thigh bone and lower leg bones.

At the top of your skeleton is your skull, an amazingly strong structure made from twenty-two different bones that lock together like a 3D jigsaw. Your brain is protected by the frontal bone, as well as the parietal and temporal bones.

Nasal bones form the bridge of your nose, but the end is made up of cartilage rather than bone. This is why skeletons don't have noses.

QUIZ

How much does the average adult's skeleton weigh?

A. The same as one car tyre.
B. The same as five BMX bikes.
C. The same as fifteen bricks.

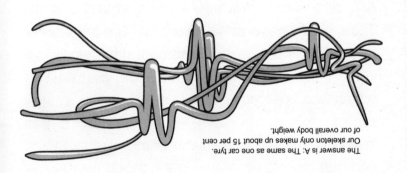

The answer is A: The same as one car tyre.
Our skeleton only makes up about 15 per cent
of our overall body weight.

Your upper jaw, or maxilla, is made up of two bones that fuse together beneath your nose. Your lower jaw, or mandible, is the only moveable part of the skull.

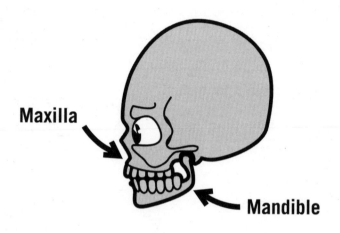

Maxilla

Mandible

A baby's skull is not fully formed when it's born. Their skulls have small gaps which allows them to stretch as the brain grows. But don't worry – if you are old enough to read this book, your skull no longer has any gaps.

You have three bones in your arm: the ulna, radius and humerus. If you have ever banged your elbow you'll know how it feels all tingly when you do. That's why people call it the funny bone. But what you've really done is bump you ulnar nerve where it is unprotected by bone. So not only is your funny bone not especially funny, it's not even a bone.

Your ribcage is strong, and guards vital body parts such as your heart. Your hip bone, or pelvis, supports the organs in your abdomen and anchors your legs.

Your feet contain many small bones like the metatarsals that most people only find out the names of when their favourite footballers get injured.

DID YOU KNOW?

Your thigh bone, or femur, is the longest bone in your body, accounting for a quarter of your height.

XAND: Although your bones are strong, they're not entirely solid. Inside your largest bones is a substance called bone marrow, which is like jelly.

CHRIS: Except that it doesn't come in a range of delicious flavours, or go very well with ice cream.

XAND: It's not that much like jelly, come to think of it. But it is softer than your bones.

Your Joints

CHRIS: Bones are held together by joints. Joints allow the bones to move around with flexibility.

XAND: We should all be grateful for joints because without them, all sports would consist of people standing around awkwardly and not moving.

CHRIS: Season ticket holders would be livid.

DID YOU KNOW?

You are one centimetre taller in the morning than in the evening. This is because the soft cartilage between your bones gets compressed by your daily activities.

OPERATION OUCH!

XAND: The body contains around 350 joints. Some of them bring together just two bones, while some, such as the wrist and ankle, join several together. Not all joints can move. For example, the bones in your skull are held together by strong, fixed joints.

CHRIS: You can help keep your bones strong by drinking milk, which is rich in calcium. Sadly ice cream doesn't really count because it's also full of fat and sugar.

XAND: Healthy bones are very strong and can withstand a lot of force.

CHRIS: I hope you'll never be unlucky enough to break one of your bones, but if you are, the doctors in your local hospital can help it to heal.

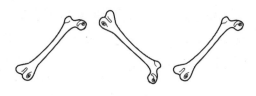

Bone injuries

A break or a crack in a bone is known as a fracture. A clean fracture is the name for a break that doesn't damage surrounding tissue. A compound fracture is the name for a break that damages tissue or even breaks through the skin. Ouch!

Doctors often take an X-ray to find out if you have a fracture. They might need to push the bone back into position before holding it in place with a plaster cast. Double ouch!

Your body can mend broken bones, but it's a very gradual process that can take a few weeks or months. At least it gives your friends plenty of time to sign the plaster cast.

YOUR MUSCLES →

XAND: As you might know, I have super strength, but I don't like to talk about it.

CHRIS: Or prove it in any way.

XAND: But even if you don't have my special powers, your muscles still do an amazingly complicated job.

DID YOU KNOW?

The biggest muscle in your body is in your bum, and it's called the gluteus maximus. The smallest is in your ear, and it's called the stapedius. It's just over one millimetre long.

There are more than six hundred muscles in the body. Bodybuilders might seem to have more, but they have the same muscles as everybody else – only much bigger.

As you might expect, your muscles help you run, jump and curl in an amazing free kick from outside the penalty area in the last minute of stoppage time. But did you know they also help you talk, eat, blink, breathe and look slightly puzzled in maths lessons?

There are more than fifty muscles in your face, and you use them to let people know if you're happy, sad, scared or surprised.

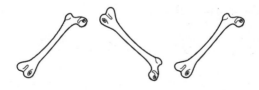

XAND: You're probably wondering why I have much bigger muscles than most people.

CHRIS: No, I'm wondering why you always ask me to help you carry the shopping.

DID YOU KNOW?

You use two hundred of the six hundred muscles in your body when you take a step, and almost all of them when you throw a ball.

Each of your muscles is made up of thousands of tiny fibres. When bodybuilders lift heavy weights, small tears appear in them. This makes their bodies build the fibres back bigger and stronger than before.

Muscles can *pull* parts of your body, but they can't *push* them. This is why many muscles are arranged in opposing pairs. For example, the muscles in our upper arms are known as the biceps and triceps.

The biceps and triceps work together to move the lower arm. When the biceps shortens, it pulls the lower arm up. When the triceps shortens, it pulls the lower arm down.

To move one of your muscles, your brain sends a small electrical charge down a nerve. In our lab we attached electricity-conducting pads directly to Chris's muscles to gain some control over them. Obviously this falls firmly into the 'don't try this at home' category.

Even very simple movements require complicated combinations of muscles. Picking up this book and reading it requires a complex interaction of

your hand, wrist, shoulder, arm, eye, head and neck muscles. And your mouth, of course, as you mutter the words 'Woah!' and 'That's brilliant!' over and over again.

Muscle Problems

Muscle problems can be very painful. A muscle strain is caused when a muscle is pulled so hard that fibres get damaged. Ouch! Sometimes the fibres are stretched so hard they break, which is known as a muscle tear. Double ouch!

BODY TRICKS: Clockwise and Anticlockwise

CHRIS: Here's a trick that will stop your friends from being able to control the movements of their feet.

XAND: They'll be completely under your power and do exactly as you please. Mwah ha ha!

CHRIS: Not quite. But it will make them slightly confused. Tell a friend to sit down and move their right foot in a clockwise circle.

XAND: While they're doing this, ask them to trace a number six in the air with their right index finger.

CHRIS: Your friend's brain will be bamboozled, and they won't be able to do both at once.

XAND: *Aaarrggh!* Brain melt!

CHRIS: The parts of your brain that control movement can't cope with two opposite movements at the same time.

XAND: In this trick, you're asking your friend to move their foot clockwise and their hand anticlockwise.

CHRIS: It's too much for their poor little brain to cope with, so they either change the direction of their foot, or give up altogether.

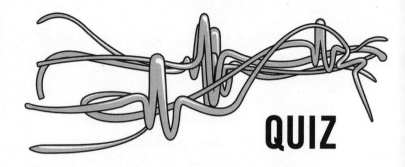

QUIZ

What is the body's largest organ?

A. Your heart.
B. Your lungs.
C. Your skin.

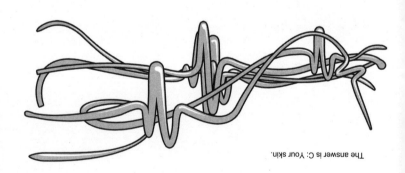

The answer is C: Your skin.

YOUR LUNGS →

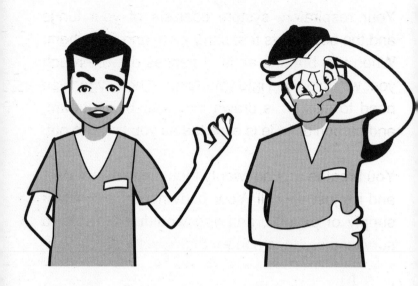

CHRIS: Take a deep breath and let it out again. Doesn't that feel great?

XAND: It depends where you are, of course. If you're in a meadow in summer, then yes. If you're in the school toilets, then no.

CHRIS: Whether that was a nice experience or not, it was all thanks to your respiratory system.

Your respiratory system consists of your lungs and the body parts that carry air to and from them. When you breathe air in, it passes down through your windpipe and into your lungs. The oxygen you need to survive is drawn into your bloodstream, and carbon dioxide is expelled as you breathe out.

You breathe around twenty thousand times a day, and it's just as well. Your body needs a constant supply of oxygen, and you wouldn't be able to survive more than a few minutes without it.

Luckily, you breathe automatically. It would get very annoying if you had to remind yourself to do it twenty thousand times a day.

Xand's to-do list:
Breathe in
Breathe out
Buy milk
Breathe in
Breathe out
Go to work
Breathe in
Breathe out

THAT'S BRILLIANT

Shaun Jones has such powerful lungs he can make a hot water bottle explode. Blowing up a thick plastic hot water bottle is fifty times harder than blowing up a party balloon, but Shaun can do it because he has the ability to expand his lungs more than the average person. He inflates his amazing lungs, pushes his diaphragm up and blows air out with extraordinary force.

Several important muscles are used as we breathe. Your intercostal muscles are located between your ribs, and these are used to move your ribcage up and down. Your diaphragm is located underneath your lungs and it contracts to increase the size of your lungs so you can draw air in.

CHRIS: Try breathing in . . .

XAND: What's just happened is that your diaphragm and intercostals have contracted so that your lungs can stretch.

CHRIS: Now breathe out . . .

XAND: Your diaphragm and intercostals have relaxed and your lungs have shrunk again, forcing air out through your nose.

Even if you aren't in the school toilets, the air may still contain nasty stuff. If you live in a city you probably breathe in loads of dirt every day. But don't worry, because your heroic snot saves you by trapping dust. This is why it goes black if you're in an especially polluted place.

DID YOU KNOW?

It's often said that humans have five senses, which are sight, hearing, touch, taste and smell. We even talk about spooky powers such as telepathy as a sixth sense. But we have additional senses, such as our sense of heat and its absence, our sense of balance, our sense of pain and our sense of body position.

QUIZ

How many hot water bottles could you fill with one day's worth of breathing?

A. Two hundred and fifty
B. Seven hundred and fifty
C. One thousand

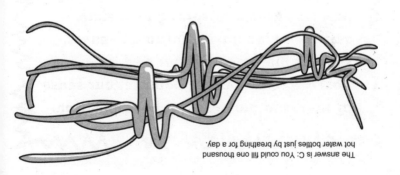

The answer is C: You could fill one thousand hot water bottles just by breathing for a day.

BODY TRICKS: *Against the Wall*

XAND: Here's a trick that will stop your friends from being able to move their feet.

CHRIS: And it's all done using mind control powers.

XAND: Not really. There's actually a simple scientific explanation.

CHRIS: Get your friend to put their left foot flat against the wall so that the side of their shoe is touching it.

XAND: Then get them to put their left ear against the wall too.

CHRIS: Now ask them to lift their right foot.

XAND: They won't be able to, unless they cheat and sneak their other foot away from the wall.

CHRIS: To lift your right leg above the ground, you'd need to shift your weight directly above your left leg to keep your body balanced.

XAND: But in this case the wall gets in the way, so you can't lift your right foot at all.

CHRIS: It's all very simple, really.

XAND: You can still pretend you did it with mind control powers if you like.

YOUR HEART →

OPERATION OUCH!

XAND: You might think that hearts are soppy things that people draw on valentine cards.

CHRIS: But your heart is actually an amazing non-stop machine that pumps blood around your body at incredible speed.

XAND: See? Not so soppy after all, is it?

Your heart works constantly to pump blood around your body, supplying it with oxygen, energy and nutrients. Blood pumps out of the heart at forty centimetres per second.

Your heart is made up of two very powerful pumps. One sends blood to your lungs while the other sends it around the rest of your body.

Your heart can pump all the blood in your body in just one minute. It could pump enough blood to fill a large swimming pool every month. It wouldn't be a very nice swimming pool, though. Hardly anyone would want to dive in, and those who did would look disgusting when they got out.

Even while you're happily snoozing away, your hard-working heart keeps on squirting blood around your body. It will pump away twenty-four hours a day for the rest of your life.

XAND: It might seem strange that such a powerful organ should be associated with greetings cards and love letters.

CHRIS: The heart only appears on valentine cards because we used to think it controlled emotions. We now know the brain is responsible, but the tradition of using the heart to represent love continues to this day.

Your Heartbeat

Your heart muscles contract to send blood around your body and relax to let more blood flow in. This creates your heartbeat, which doctors can listen to with an instrument known as a stethoscope.

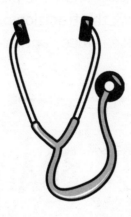

Blood is carried away from your heart by blood vessels called arteries and brought back to it by blood vessels called veins. As blood surges through the arteries, it makes them bulge slightly. This creates your pulse, which medical staff will sometimes check to find out how quickly blood is flowing around your body.

You've got a pulse right now. Unless you're dead, in which case we're sorry to hear about your condition.

137

You can check the pulse in your wrist by holding you palm upwards and putting your first and middle finger on the inside of your wrist, at the base of your thumb. Then press your skin lightly until you can feel your pulse. Count how many times it beats in a minute to find your resting heart rate.

Your resting heart rate will probably fall between seventy and one hundred beats per minute, depending on your age. When you exercise, you'll find that your heartbeat increases. This is because your muscles need more oxygen, so your heart has to supply them with blood more quickly. People who are very fit, such as professional athletes, often have a lower than average resting heart rate.

XAND: Watch out, Chris! There's a flesh-eating monster right behind you!

CHRIS: **Help! Run!**

XAND: Not really. I was just demonstrating that your heart rate increases when you're scared. And it's all down to something called adrenaline.

CHRIS: **Except in this case my heart rate didn't increase, because I didn't fall for it.**

Your Adrenaline

Adrenaline is a hormone that helps your body respond to danger by increasing your heart rate and blood flow. This lets you attack or run away, and is known as the 'fight or flight' response.

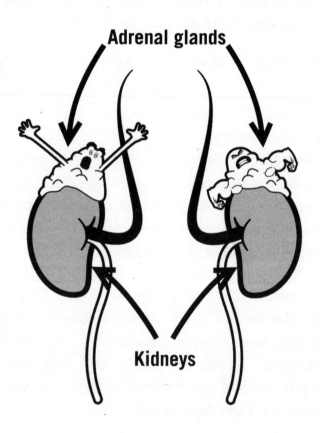

Adrenal glands

Kidneys

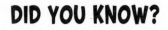

DID YOU KNOW?

In extreme cases it's actually possible to scare someone to death. Sometimes so much adrenaline is released into the body that it causes fatal damage to the heart.

If you go on a scary roller coaster, you'll notice the effects of adrenaline. At first your heart rate is normal, but then the ride tricks your body into thinking you're in real danger. Your body releases adrenaline because it thinks you're going to need to fight or run away. Neither of which would be a very clever idea on a roller coaster.

Your heart rate is very high when you finish the ride, but then it goes up even further. This is because your body is pleased it's survived the dangerous situation. Sometimes this makes people want to go straight to the back of the queue and start the ride again.

But once you've survived the experience, it will be harder to trick your body into thinking you're in danger, so you might not get the same reaction. This is why roller coaster fans are constantly seeking higher, faster and scarier rides.

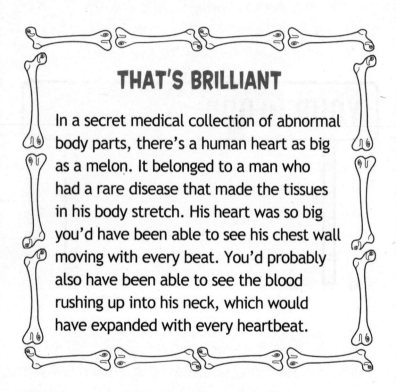

THAT'S BRILLIANT

In a secret medical collection of abnormal body parts, there's a human heart as big as a melon. It belonged to a man who had a rare disease that made the tissues in his body stretch. His heart was so big you'd have been able to see his chest wall moving with every beat. You'd probably also have been able to see the blood rushing up into his neck, which would have expanded with every heartbeat.

YOUR BLOOD →

CHRIS: Some people think blood is a bit disgusting.

XAND: But the truth is, your blood is essential and without it you'd die.

CHRIS: So it's not disgusting at all. It's brilliant.

DID YOU KNOW?

Around four thousand litres of blood are needed in hospitals every day. People who donate it help to save millions of lives each year. Their bodies will make up for the donated blood in a few days.

Adults have about five litres of blood in their bodies. It's made up of three main types of blood cell. Red blood cells give the fluid its colour. They take oxygen from the lungs and carry it around the body. White blood cells fight disease and help to remove waste from the body. The other type is known as platelets and they help the blood to clot.

Not everyone has the same sort of blood. There are four different blood groups, which are labelled A, B, AB and O. These are further divided into positive and negative. In the United Kingdom, the most common blood type is O+, followed by A+, B+ and O-. Blood groups are very important to doctors, who need to know what type someone is before performing a transfusion, and vampires, who prefer type B.

OK, so that last bit isn't true.

CHRIS: Your blood flows constantly around your body all the time with amazing speed.

XAND: This is why your blood would spurt everywhere if your head was bitten off by a giant monster.

CHRIS: This next bit of the book will help you understand what's going on if you ever find yourself in this situation.

When blood pumps out of your heart, it travels through a network of blood vessels. The three types of blood vessels are known as arteries, capillaries and veins. Blood first travels down arteries, which have a strong layer of muscle in their walls to push the blood along.

If you look at your wrist, you can probably see your veins under the skin. Some people find it strange that their veins look blue. The reason for this is to do with the way your skin absorbs light and reflects it back to your eye. You don't actually have any blue blood. Even if you're in the royal family.

GROSS OUT

Leeches are a type of worm with thirty-two brains that love to feed on blood. Although you might assume doctors stopped using them in the Middle Ages, they're actually still used today. Their saliva releases a chemical that stops blood from clotting, and doctors can use them for healing skin grafts and restoring circulation. They might be greedy and gross, but they're amazing little healers and they might help to save your life one day.

Blood Problems

Sometimes people have problems with their blood because of the things they eat. Fatty foods can clog the lining of arteries, making things like blood clots more likely. Salt and sugar can raise blood pressure, which can increase the risk of getting some diseases.

On the other hand, eating foods that contain a lot of iron can help to keep red blood cells healthy. Good news if you love things like fish, beef, lamb and beans. Bad news if you prefer fries and fizzy drinks. Boo!

DID YOU KNOW?

There are over 161,000 kilometres of blood vessels in your brain. That means if you laid them out in line they would stretch around the world four times!

YOUR HANDS →

XAND: Let's have a big hand for your hands.

CHRIS: Just think of all the things they help you with. Writing, texting, eating, catching, carrying, playing computer games.

XAND: Thanks, hands!

Your hands are amazingly flexible thanks to their complex framework of bones and the network of muscles and tendons that cover them.

Each of your hands is made up of twenty-seven bones, and together they account for over a quarter of the bones in your body.

CHRIS: One of the reasons you can hold this book right now is because you've got opposable thumbs.

XAND: Your pets don't have them. Unless you have a pet chimpanzee.

CHRIS: In which case why not get it to hold the book open for you as you read?

Along with other primates such as apes, humans have opposable thumbs, which we can press against our fingers, allowing us to handle objects and use tools. Meanwhile, animals without opposable thumbs such as cats and dogs have to look on jealously as we open cans of food for them.

The tips of your fingers have more than three thousand touch sensors per square centimetre, and are among the most sensitive areas of your body. As the sensors are squashed by the things you touch, they change shape and send messages to your brain.

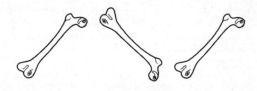

XAND: Some animals, such as koalas, also have unique fingerprints.

CHRIS: It's worth remembering that if there's a break-in at your local eucalyptus leaf factory.

XAND: That's right. They might look cute and cuddly, but that's no reason for them to escape justice.

The stiff nails on the back of your fingers protect them and help you grip things. Nails are made of keratin, the same substance as your hair and the outer layer of your skin. As with hair and skin, the part of the nail you can see is dead. The only living part is the root, which is under your skin.

Most people keep their nails short, but there are some people who let them grow as long as possible. An Indian man called Shridhar Chillal grew the nails on his left hand until they were a total of six metres long. Fortunately, the nails on his right hand are of normal length, so he doesn't have to go outside and ask for help every time he has an itchy nose.

DID YOU KNOW?

Your fingernails grow quicker than your toenails. This is partly because your hands have better blood circulation than your feet.

People who can perform tasks better with their right hand are known as right-handed. Those who perform them better with their left hand are known as left-handed. People who can do tasks equally well with either hand are called ambidextrous.

Studies have estimated that around 90 per cent of people are right-handed, and just 10 per cent of people are left-handed, while truly ambidextrous people are very rare.

DID YOU KNOW?

Your body contains two different types of muscle fibre. The first are called fast twitch fibres and they contract quickly, but get tired easily. The second are called slow twitch fibres and they contract slowly, but can keep going for much longer. Long distance runners are likely to have more slow twitch fibres. Sprinters are likely to have more fast twitch fibres.

BODY TRICKS: The Incredible Shrinking Arm

CHRIS: Here's a trick that will make your friend's arms shrink.

XAND: What? This doesn't involve witchcraft, does it? If it does, I want no part of it.

CHRIS: No. Just simple science. Get your friend to put their fingertips together and hold their arms out as far as they'll go.

XAND: OK, I'm doing it.

CHRIS: Now tell them to rub their other arm with one of their hands.

XAND: OK. Give me a minute.

CHRIS: While they're doing this, pretend you're using your magic powers to shorten their arm.

XAND: Careful. Don't use too much magic!

CHRIS: After they've been doing it for about a minute, tell them to straighten their arms again. One of them will now be shorter than the other.

XAND: *Aaarggh!* What's happened?

CHRIS: It's easy to make them the same size again. Just rub your other elbow with your other hand.

XAND: OK . . .

CHRIS: The trick works because the muscles in your arm tighten up as you rub your elbow. This makes it appear shorter than your other arm, which is relaxed. When you use your other arm, it tenses up too, making them both appear the same size again.

XAND: Now both my arms are short. If I keep this up any longer, I won't be able to reach my pockets.

CHRIS: It's fine. Just give your arms a good shake and they'll return to normal.

XAND: Phew!

YOUR STOMACH →

CHRIS: It's about time we started talking about food.

XAND: Why? Is it lunch?

CHRIS: No. It's the section on the stomach. Lunch isn't for a few more minutes.

XAND: Bah!

When you pop a piece of your favourite food in your mouth, you send it on a dark journey that lasts over a day and ends in your bottom. Which doesn't sound like a very nice way to treat something you're fond of.

DID YOU KNOW?

As well as making you sick, bacteria can also get sick themselves. They can be invaded by a type of virus known as a bacteria eater.

Food is chewed by your teeth and travels down your oesophagus into your stomach, then through your small and large intestines, rectum and anus into (hopefully) the toilet. The collective name for all these things is the digestive tract. As food travels through your body, it is broken down. Your body absorbs what it needs and expels the rest as waste.

CHRIS: The journey starts when you pop a bit of delicious food in your mouth.

XAND: I wish we'd done this bit after lunch. It's making me feel hungry.

DID YOU KNOW?

You get a new stomach lining every three to four days. It would dissolve if it weren't constantly replaced, due to the strong acid in your stomach. In other words, it would digest itself. *Eww!*

You use your teeth to crush the food up and make it easy to swallow. It mixes with the saliva produced by your mouth to create a mushy pulp.

Saliva is produced by glands on either side of your mouth. It contains a substance known as amylase, which breaks down food.

Saliva is a very impressive and useful substance. Although it's less impressive if you let it drool out of the side of your mouth while you stare longingly into the cake shop window.

DID YOU KNOW?

The amylase in your saliva breaks down starches. It's the same thing that's used in detergents to clean stains on clothes. It's not a very good idea to spit on your clothes instead of washing them, though.

Your tongue forces the food into your upper throat as you swallow. A flap called the epiglottis covers the entrance to your windpipe to make sure the food doesn't go down there and make you choke. The food then travels down your oesophagus into your stomach.

Chemicals in your stomach such as hydrochloric acid start to break down food as soon as it enters. Foods tend to stay in your stomach for one to four hours, though fatty foods can stay longer. To help keep the food in until it's ready to leave, the entrance and exit of the stomach are surrounded by rings of muscle known as sphincters.

GROSS OUT

Lots of people find that if someone near them throws up, they can't stop themselves vomiting too. Some scientists reckon this goes back to the days when humans used to share food in large groups. If someone started vomiting, it was a sign that the food might be poisoned and everyone else should spew it up as well. *Bleeuuurrgghh!*

Food leaves your stomach as a thick, dark mush and enters your small intestine, which is a long, coiled tube in your lower body. This continues breaking the food down and absorbing nutrients.

Next, your large intestine removes water and the last remaining nutrients from the food matter and pushes the waste into a short tube called the rectum. It is then squeezed out of the double ring of muscles known as your anus and into the toilet.

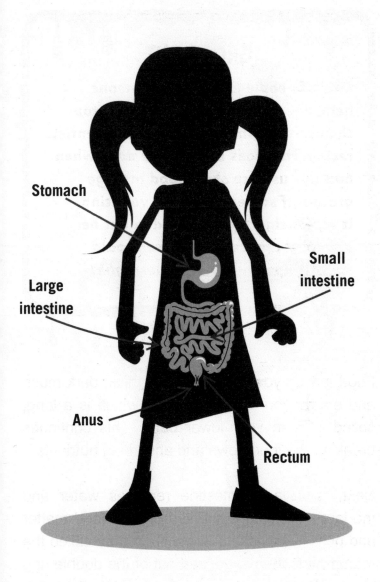

Stomach

Small intestine

Large intestine

Anus

Rectum

OPERATION OUCH!

The delicious food you popped in your mouth has now been broken down over a journey of nine metres into soggy pulp, dark brown mush and, finally, fresh poo.

CHRIS: So, should we get lunch now?

XAND: Actually, I don't feel very hungry any more.

DID YOU KNOW?

The noise that most people think is their stomach rumbling is actually gas and fluid passing through the intestines. It has the wonderful scientific name of borborygmus.

Stomach pain is very common. People often get a stomach ache if they wolf down their food without chewing it properly, swallowing large chunks that are difficult to digest. They can also swallow too much air, making them burp or fart later on, which will make those around them suffer too.

BODY TRICKS: *Mind Reading*

CHRIS: This trick will convince your friends you can read their minds.

XAND: Give a penny to your friend and tell them to put it in one of their hands while you look away.

CHRIS: While you're still looking away, tell them to lift the hand holding the penny above their head.

XAND: Now tell them to put their hands back together, fists closed, and turn around to look at them.

CHRIS: Look down at their hands and pretend to use your mind-reading powers.

XAND: The hand with the penny in will be easy to spot because the veins on the back of it won't be sticking up as much.

CHRIS: That's because the blood will have drained out when they stuck their hand in the air.

XAND: Meanwhile your friend will gasp in awe at your mind-reading powers and declare you the coolest person in the universe.

CHRIS: Soon the entire world will bow before you with respect and fear.

XAND: Until they get hold of this book and work out how you did the trick.

YOUR PANCREAS →

CHRIS: The pancreas is unlikely to feature in anyone's list of top ten organs.

XAND: It hardly ever gets the same amount of attention as more high-profile bits like the brain, the eyes and the nose. Even the kidneys have a bigger fanbase.

CHRIS: But we thought we'd include it as a stop on our tour so it doesn't feel left out.

Your pancreas is located between your stomach and your spine, with your small intestine looped around it. It releases pancreatic fluid into your small intestine, which helps with your digestion.

Pancreatic fluid helps break down protein, starch and fat, so they can be absorbed by your body. At the same time, an organ called your gall bladder squirts a yellow liquid called bile into your small intestine, helping to break down fat.

So, as you can see, the modest pancreas deserves a little TLC.

GROSS OUT

You are currently covered in thousands of tiny living organisms. *Eww!* Fortunately, this is completely normal. *Yay!* The organisms are called bacteria and can sometimes be very helpful. For example, some live in your gut and help you digest food, while others can help you fight disease.

YOUR LIVER →

CHRIS: Your liver is another organ that doesn't get the recognition it deserves.

XAND: Not only is your liver the largest organ on the inside of your body, but it performs over five hundred functions.

CHRIS: Well it's time to give this workaholic organ the attention it deserves.

Your liver is found in the middle of your abdomen. It's divided into a large right lobe and a smaller left lobe.

It removes poisons from your blood, stores sugar, fats, copper, iron and vitamins, makes digestive juices, regulates cholesterol and gets rid of old red blood cells. It would probably make you dinner and help you with your homework too if you asked nicely. That's how hard-working it is.

All of this activity produces heat, and keeping your body warm is yet another incredibly useful thing your liver does for you. And does it get a word of thanks? No.

Another awesome thing about the liver is that it can regenerate itself. Even if you lost three quarters of your liver, the bit that remained could grow into a new one.

Despite this amazing quality, some people still have problems with their livers. And given all the work the poor organ does, it's no surprise that these problems can be very serious.

Sometimes doctors perform liver transplants. This is where an unhealthy liver is removed from someone's body and replaced with a healthy liver from someone who's recently died.

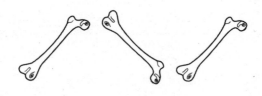

THAT'S BRILLIANT

Paul Hunn holds the world record for the loudest burp. One of his belches measured 109.9 decibels. That's as loud as a car horn or motorbike. He discovered his talent during burping contests in the playground when he was at school. He prepares for burping events by drawing lots of air in through his mouth.

BODY TRICKS: *Wall Moving*

CHRIS: Here's a great body trick that will convince your friends you've got the power to move walls.

XAND: Get a friend to stand facing a wall with their arms straight and their fingertips touching it.

CHRIS: Then get them to move their arms round backwards in big circles.

XAND: While they're doing this, pretend you're pushing the wall away from them with your amazing strength.

CHRIS: When they've done a few circles, ask them to touch the wall again.

XAND: They won't be able to, but it won't really be because of your wall-moving powers.

CHRIS: It happens because the muscles in their shoulders will tighten up while they're moving their arms round in circles.

XAND: Things might get a bit tricky if they ask you to push the wall again without them circling their arms.

CHRIS: Just explain that you have to use your wall-moving powers responsibly, because you don't want the whole building to collapse.

YOUR BOTTOM →

CHRIS: All right, stop sniggering at the back. Your bottom is a part of your body like any other, and deserves to be taken seriously.

XAND: Tee hee! He said 'bottom'.

CHRIS: If it weren't for your bottom, you'd have no way to get rid of waste matter from your body.

XAND: Tee hee! He's talking about poo.

Your rectum is a short tube at the bottom of your large intestine. Poo collects there until it's ready to be expelled through your anus. More than half of your poo is likely to be water, with undigested food material making up the rest.

Poo is usually brown due to something called bilirubin that comes from dead red blood cells. Sometimes poo changes colour, and it's often because of something you've eaten, like beetroot, liquorice or blueberries. However, if your poo stays too black, too white or too reddish, it's a good idea to see your doctor.

Healthy poo is often shaped like a sausage, but it can appear in separate hard lumps if you have constipation. At the other extreme, your poo can go very runny if you have diarrhoea, which can be a sign of infection such as food poisoning. Or it might just mean that you've eaten some food that was too spicy.

CHRIS: You can make the time you spend on the toilet quicker and easier if you eat the right kinds of food.

XAND: That's right. Next time you're about to scoff some sugary cereal, try eating some that's high in bran instead. Your bottom would thank you if it could.

DID YOU KNOW?

In your lifetime, you'll spend a total of one year sitting on the toilet. Not all at once, obviously. Unless your diet is *very* bad.

You can make it easier to poo by eating foods that are high in fibre, such as fruit, vegetables, nuts and bran cereals. If you eat a high-fibre diet, your poo will be more solid. It will glide through your digestive system and plop easily into your toilet.

But if you eat an unhealthy, low-fibre diet, your body will find it harder to push it through your digestive system and it will sit there for ages. Just like you will on the toilet.

CHRIS: While we're here, we should probably mention the subject of breaking wind.

XAND: However, just because it's mentioned in this book, doesn't give you the right to let rip in class and claim you're doing a science experiment.

GROSS OUT

Ever spotted a piece of sweetcorn in your poo? It's because your body can't break down the outer shell, because it doesn't have the right enzyme. It can digest the inner part of the sweetcorn kernel though, and the outer shell is still good for fibre. So you weren't completely wasting your time when you chose it for dinner.

Flatulence, also known as farting, honking, trouser trumpeting and cutting the cheese, is what happens when you expel gasses such as methane that are trapped in your gut. It's very common, and something that everyone experiences regularly, except for members of the royal family.

When you swallow food or water, you also swallow bits of air. Gasses such as methane are added to it as you digest food. Your body needs to get rid of this excess of gas, so your bottom expels it.

The average number of trumps is said to be fifteen a day, though sometimes people do a lot more because they've eaten food that's difficult to digest. Some examples are beans, cabbage, lentils, cauliflower, prunes and brussel sprouts.

Extreme flatulence can also be a symptom of problems such as constipation and irritable bowel syndrome.

You can cut down on your chances of embarrassing flatulence by eating foods that are easier to digest, such as potatoes, rice, lettuce, bananas, oranges and grapes. You should also take care to eat your food slowly and avoid chewing gum, to reduce the amount of air you swallow.

Obviously, you should increase your intake of beans and sprouts if you want to increase your flatulence for some weird reason. Just don't blame us if no one sits next to you in class.

Believe it or not, professional guffing is a tradition that goes back hundreds of years. Famous flatulists include Le Petomane, who performed in nineteenth century France, and Roland the Farter, a jester from the twelfth century.

THAT'S BRILLIANT

Paul Oldfield from Macclesfield in Cheshire, also known as Mr Methane, makes his living as a professional farter. He's mastered the art of trumping and can let one rip whenever he wants. He expands the muscles in his bum, draws air in by raising his diaphragm and then expels it by contracting the muscles.

YOUR BLADDER →

XAND: The toilet break isn't quite over yet, because now it's time to turn our attention to another bodily function.

CHRIS: We're talking about number ones here. Relieving yourself. Having a wee, or a tinkle. You get the idea.

GROSS OUT

Ever wondered why your wee changes colour? Sometimes it's almost clear, other times it's orange. It's all to do with how much water you drink and how much you sweat. If you've been drinking enough water, your wee should be clear or light yellow. If it's darker, you need to drink more. This can happen when the weather is hot, and you haven't been drinking enough extra water to make up for the fluids you're losing by sweating.

The average amount of water in the adult human body is about 60 per cent. Every day, we lose and gain about 2.85 litres of water. As you might expect, most of it comes from the liquids we drink, but quite a lot also comes from food. We lose some water through sweat, some through vapour breathed out of our lungs, a little through pooing and a lot through weeing.

The truth is weeing is very important for your body. Your parents might get annoyed when they have to stop at every single motorway service station on a long journey because you drank too much squash, but they should be glad your urinary system is in good working order.

XAND: We get rid of about 1.85 litres of urine a day. That's about enough to fill a bath every month.

CHRIS: *Eww!* I'm not going near that bath! It sounds disgusting!

XAND: I'm not talking about a real bath. It was just to show how much wee we do.

Your urinary system is made up of two bean-shaped kidneys, two tubes called ureters and your bladder, which holds urine until it's ready to pass out of the body.

Your kidneys are constantly processing your blood and extracting waste substances and surplus water to create urine, which is then passed on to your bladder.

GROSS OUT

Your wee contains ammonia, which is also used for cleaning. This is why Ancient Romans sometimes washed their tunics in wee. That must have smelt nice on a hot day.

Your bladder is small and wrinkled when empty, but its muscular walls stretch as it fills up with urine. You'll feel the need to go to the toilet when it's got about 0.2 litres of urine in it, although it can hold much more than that.

Stretch sensors in the wall of the bladder tell your brain it's time to go to the toilet, and you ask your parents to stop the car, put your hand up in class or bang on the door of the bathroom and tell your sister to hurry up, depending on the situation.

GROSS OUT

Some foods like garlic and asparagus can make your pee smell. Asparagus contains lots of asparagusic acid. When you digest asparagusic acid, it releases the horrible smell associated with asparagus urine.

YOUR GENES →

CHRIS: We've almost reached the end of our journey. But there's one very important part of the body we haven't mentioned yet.

XAND: Is it that weird fold of skin in the corner of our eyes?

CHRIS: No. It's our genes. Not to be confused with our jeans, which are actually removable and not part of our body at all.

Every single thing about you, from the colour of your skin to the shape of your nose to the curliness of your hair, is determined by a set of instructions inside your body, called genes.

All this information is written on tiny strands called DNA. These are arranged in a shape that looks like a twisty ladder. Our bodies contain a huge amount of DNA. If you could unravel all the DNA in your body it would reach the moon *six thousand* times.

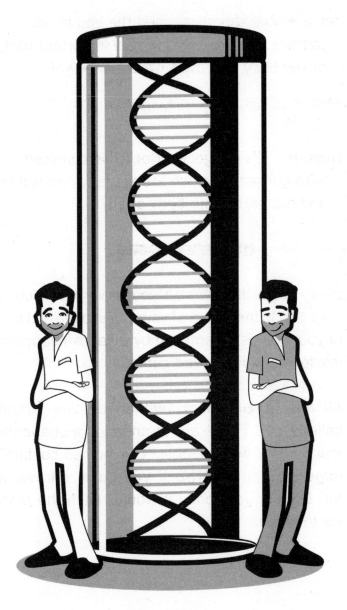

Half the information in your genes comes from your mum and the other half comes from your dad, which is why you probably look a bit like both parents. If you've ever endured a long family conversation about whether you look more like your mum or your dad, you'll know all about this already.

DID YOU KNOW?

The DNA of several important people including scientist Stephen Hawking is stored on the international space station. It's supposed to help rebuild the human race if the earth is destroyed.

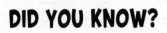

DID YOU KNOW?

You share over 95 per cent of your DNA with a chimpanzee. We don't just mean you personally. It's true of all humans.

CHRIS: As identical twins, we share virtually the same genes.

XAND: Except that I got more coolness genes, of course.

CHRIS: Please take no notice. Scientists have never discovered a coolness gene.

XAND: That's because they haven't studied me.

CHRIS: Some people think that identical twins share some sort of psychic link.

XAND: However, whenever I try to guess what Xand is thinking, I usually get it wrong.

CHRIS: Although to be fair, sometimes your guesses do rhyme.

YOUR TOES →

CHRIS: And so we come to the end of our amazing journey at your feet.

XAND: You probably don't think about them much except for when you're buying new shoes, but your feet are incredibly complicated and hard-working.

CHRIS: Just think of all the walking, running, jumping and kicking you make them do every day. The poor things must be very tired.

There are over one hundred muscles, tendons and ligaments in each of your feet. These allow your feet to carry out the complicated movements needed to keep your body balanced.

Your feet have to take the weight of your whole body, so if you have problems with them it can be really uncomfortable. This is why it's important to make sure shoes are comfortable before buying them.

On the end of your toes are your toenails. Like your fingernails, they're made of keratin, and the bit you can see is dead. Keratin is made from the same substance as your pet's claws. Theirs have evolved to be sharper than ours to help them catch prey. Although now they probably use them for ruining your furniture.

GROSS OUT

You have more than 250,000 sweat glands on each foot, more than anywhere else in your body. This is why it's so important to change your socks every day. And don't leave your sweaty PE socks in your locker over the summer holidays. *Eww!*

QUIZ

How many bones are there in each of your feet?

- A. Twelve
- B. Eighteen
- C. Twenty-six

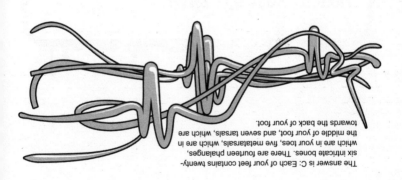

The answer is C: Each of your feet contains twenty-six intricate bones. There are fourteen phalanges, which are in your toes, five metatarsals, which are in the middle of your foot, and seven tarsals, which are towards the back of your foot.

YOUR APPENDIX →

CHRIS: Look how clever and funny we are! We're putting the section on your appendix at the back of the book. Exactly where you'd find a book's appendix!

XAND: And like this chapter, your appendix is a pretty pointless addition to your body.

Your appendix is a small closed tube on the end of your large intestine. It serves no purpose in the digestive system, though some believe it's left over from the days when humans used to eat things that are difficult to digest, such as leaves and bark.

When nicer foods such as woolly mammoth burgers came along, humans stopped bothering with all the leaves and bark, but the appendix remained.

The appendix can still get blocked and infected. If this happens it might have to be removed by doctors. Appendicitis occurs when a blockage inflames the appendix. The appendix usually has to be removed quickly, in case it bursts and causes serious infections. Ouch!

So even though it's pretty useless, the appendix can still cause us problems. Thanks, appendix! If only our ancestors had resisted all that bark.

CHRIS: And that's it! We hope you've enjoyed this tour of your body.

XAND: Your body performs amazing, astounding and sometimes slightly disgusting feats every second of every day.

CHRIS: So take care of your brilliant body to make sure it stays that way.

Acknowledgements

Many thanks to: Tim Collins, Ian France, Kez Margrie, Tamara Walton, James Gurden, Christian Welsh, Romily Menzies, Carolyn Payne, Kerry Newcombe, Miranda Sherriff, Jodie Adams, Miranda Chadwick, Kate Mander, Liza Abbott, Ben Gale, Paul Wolff, Jodie Evans, Mish Mayer, Stephen Koumas, the teams at Hamyard and Little, Brown Book Group, and all the many scientists, experts, clinicians, and above all, the patients who helped make the series and this book possible.

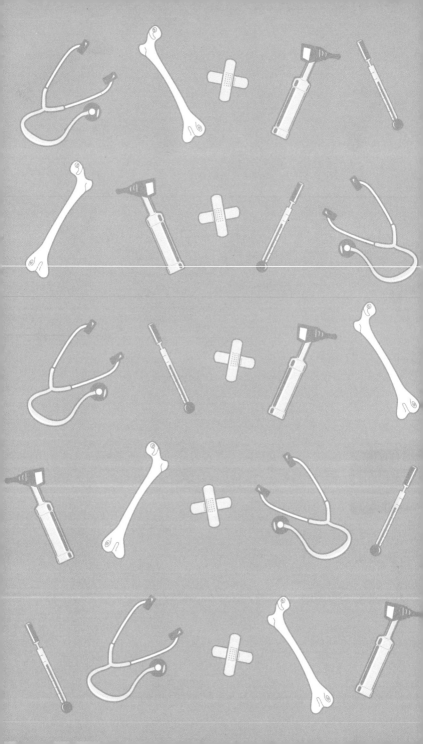